This passport contains 94 pages   *Ce passeport contient 94 pages*

PASSPORT

UNITED KINGDOM OF GREAT BRITAIN
AND NORTHERN IRELAND
ROYAUME-UNI DE GRANDE-BRETAGNE
ET D'IRLANDE DU NORD

Name of bearer }
Nom du titulaire }
HIS ROYAL HIGHNESS CHARLES PHILIP ARTHUR GEORGE THE PRINCE OF WALES

Accompanied by spouse }
Accompagné de son épouse }

and by }
et de }   { children
                  { enfants

National status }
Nationalité }
PRINCE OF THE ROYAL HOUSE.

No. of passport }
No. du passeport }
B 131415

Attention is drawn to the notes at the back of this passport

In Private - In Public
THE PRINCE AND PRINCESS OF WALES

ALASTAIR BURNET
Photographed by
TIM GRAHAM

*This book is produced with the co-operation of
Their Royal Highnesses The Prince and Princess of Wales*

SUMMIT BOOKS
New York

Published by Summit Books
A Division of Simon & Schuster, Inc.
Simon & Schuster Building, Rockefeller Center,
1230 Avenue of the Americas, New York, New York 10020
SUMMIT BOOKS and colophon are registered trademarks of
Simon & Schuster, Inc.

The publishers wish to thank Stewart Purvis
for his help in the preparation of this book

Designed by Martin Bristow
Researched by Sarah Coombe
Edited by Fiona Holman

Typeset by SX Composing Limited
Printed and bound by Printer Industria Gráfica SA,
Barcelona, Spain
D.L.: B. 29451-1986

Half-title page: Prince Charles standing at the
gate of his walled garden at Highgrove

Frontispiece: The Prince and Princess of Wales with
their two sons, Prince William and Prince Henry and
the pet rabbit on the terrace at Highgrove

Facing page: Prince Charles seated in one of the
arbours of his walled garden which he designed himself

CONTENTS

THE FAMILY AT HOME

Those invited to visit the Prince and Princess of Wales at their home in Kensington Palace, and pass through the strict security checks, are normally met by the butler, Harold Brown. But sometimes not far behind is a small boy in shirt and shorts with a firm step and slightly quizzical look on his face.

When Prince William is around the house there is always somebody with an eye on him; if it is not one of his parents, it is either Harold Brown, his nanny Barbara Barnes who has looked after him since his birth, or one of the royal protection officers. He pops up in different parts of the building, often asking people who they are and what they are doing. Or visitors may discover him in the royal equerries' office, playing with toys which his parents have been given for him.

The Prince and Princess have two homes – their apartments at Kensington Palace and their country house, Highgrove in Gloucestershire. In very approximate terms, Kensington Palace is their weekday address, and Highgrove is for weekends and summer breaks.

The office work is also divided – between Kensington Palace and Buckingham Palace. The official Office of the Prince and Princess of Wales is in the south wing of Buckingham Palace. That is where all the private secretaries, equerries and back-up staff are based. But the Prince and Princess themselves do not do

Above: The Prince of Wales' Office is in the south wing of Buckingham Palace. Although the Prince and Princess have their London home at Kensington Palace their private secretaries, equerries and back-up staff are all based at Buckingham Palace. From left to right: Lieutenant-Commander Richard Aylard, the Princess's Equerry, a lady clerk, Captain Alison Ewan, the Prince's Assistant Equerry and Lieutenant-Colonel Brian Anderson, the Prince's Equerry.

On page 6: Prince Henry at Highgrove in the summer of 1986. The young prince was then a few months short of his second birthday.
On page 7: The Princess of Wales at her desk in her sitting-room at Kensington Palace

much office work there; for one thing, the Prince does not have a desk there. So the staff often come to them a mile or so away at Kensington Palace.

It is a family home, though rather a posh one. It is also the base from which the Prince of Wales organizes his part in the public life of the country. No one knows better than he the curiosity about just what his part should be, or should be allowed to be, and just what he can allow himself to say about public issues. Many years will pass before he will become the monarch – and find himself, perhaps, with more influence but again circumscribed by what the monarch is expected to do and say, a matter on which

there is more than one opinion. So his is a training in circumspection, in setting examples, in encouraging other people's initiatives as part of his own. The job is what he makes of it himself, and he and his wife lead busy lives, working for the causes they have adopted.

The Prince says little about his ambitions; the polite, modest emphasis is invariably about getting on with the job in hand, making a contribution, however small. He has ideas, and on safe subjects, such as architecture or the environment, he voices them. Economics is something else again. But over a year of public appearances he builds up, meticulously, an intellectual framework

The dining-room at Kensington Palace is used for the large programme meetings that take place twice a year. As soon as breakfast is cleared away pens, documents and writing pads are laid out on the large, round dining-table.

of allusion and questioning and even throwaway comment that leaves a clear-enough idea in the public mind of just where he stands, or is likely to stand, on the matters of the day. He may wish he could say more, but there is a professionalism in getting away with what he does say.

The royal year reported here is a mixture of the private and the public, of big occasions and small, of speeches and conversations, of adherence to the duty and formality of royalty and the opening of new opportunities in the interstices of duty. It is a year of two persons' highly unusual working lives, of their family, and of their homes.

Kensington Palace consists of

the State Apartments, which are open to the public, and the private London homes of the Prince and Princess of Wales, Princess Margaret, Princess Alice, Duchess of Gloucester, the Duke and Duchess of Gloucester, and Prince and Princess Michael of Kent.

The Palace is very convenient for getting to and from Buckingham Palace, though some who live there find it just a little too close to cosmopolitan Kensington Gardens. The Duke of Gloucester has remarked on the noise during Ramadan: 'The Moslem children in the area get fed before sunrise and don't want to go back to bed. So they go and play in the park as early as 6 am.'

The Princess of Wales uses her sitting-room at Kensington Palace for meetings with her ladies-in-waiting and equerry. In August 1986 she had a meeting with her full-time lady-in-waiting, Miss Anne Beckwith-Smith and her equerry, Lieutenant-Commander Richard Aylard to discuss forthcoming engagements in Scotland, including a visit to a submarine, HMS Trafalgar. The lady-in-waiting and equerry outlined the draft programme for visiting the submarine and went over the 'recce' they had carried out a few days earlier. As the submarine has many steep ladders they lightheartedly discussed what the Princess should wear and agreed upon dungarees and gloves.

Apartments 8 and 9, which are now the Prince and Princess's home, are the three storeys of a house where George I and George II kept their mistresses. The house faces on to a courtyard called the Prince of Wales' Court, which was probably named after George II's unfortunate son, Prince Frederick.

The house was badly damaged by fire bombs during the Second World War and was derelict until 1975, when the Department of the Environment began repairing and restoring it. The restoration took so long that it was some months after the Prince and Princess's wedding in 1981 before it was completed. Until then they had lived in Buckingham Palace. The Prince and Princess commissioned a South African interior designer, Dudley Poplak, who opted – after discussion with them – for pastel colours such as beige and peach.

The apartments consist of a large drawing-room, a sitting-room for the Princess, a study for the Prince, a kitchen, a dining-room, bedrooms, a playroom, and accommodation for the staff. In her sitting-room, the Princess holds meetings with her ladies-in-waiting and her equerry. In the room are many of the photographs she has taken of her family.

There is also a video recorder with which she and the Prince can catch up on any of their favourite television programmes which they have missed while out on engagements. They also like to watch videos of films. This year the Prince gave American television a special interview for

transmission on the night of the Academy Awards. He said that he was an avid film watcher, especially of American films. He recalled his childhood watching television programmes such as the Lone Ranger, Wells Fargo and the Cisco Kid. Asked if he could remember the name of the Lone Ranger's Indian companion, he got Tonto right first time.

Above: Prince Henry in the garden at Highgrove, dressed as a lance-corporal of the 1st Battalion of the Parachute Regiment

Facing page: Prince William accompanied by his royal protection officer returning to Kensington Palace from his nearby nursery school. He has been attending the school on two mornings a week since September 1985.

The Princess of Wales at her desk in Kensington Palace, reading briefing notes before an engagement. No matter how many engagements she has on a particular day, the Princess always tries to arrange her diary so that she can return to the young princes in good time before they go to bed.

The Prince said that he was a great admirer of the American director Steven Spielberg, who made *E.T.* He praised Spielberg's 'incredible imagination' and ability to create extraordinary childlike images to which so many people respond. But, such are the demands on royal tact, he praised British films as well. He is patron of the British Film Institute.

The sitting-room where they sometimes watch the films is quite small and the house in general is smaller than the world might suppose. The royal dining-room has to be used for meetings, so, often, the breakfast things have to be cleared away quickly and the pens, documents and writing pads laid out. The

dinners and receptions help the Prince to meet the people involved in his charities, trusts and committees. Apart from the official ones which appear in the Court Circular, there are private dinner parties for friends and for people in whom the Prince and Princess are especially interested.

The meals are cooked by chefs who travel between Highgrove and Kensington Palace. Naturally, they know the Prince and Princess's likes and dislikes and their current favourites, but the Prince often comes up with ideas that he would like them to try.

The Princess is careful about what she eats, but friends say she can, when she wants, put away more than they do. At other times there is a similarity with the

ballet dancers from the London City Ballet, of whom she is the patron, and she has discussed the problems of staying in trim with them. The Princess and all the dancers turned their noses up at the thought of beefburger and chips. She told them that she can get very tired on public engagements but if she has something such as a piece of chocolate she can 'get through anything'.

Dotted around Kensington Palace are the souvenirs and presents from royal tours, and those for which there is not room on display are stored away. They pay particular attention to those presents which they were given for their children. The Texans who presented the Prince with a Dallas Cowboys T-shirt in the spring of 1986 might have expected it would end up in a pile of such presents in some store cupboard. In fact, Prince William proudly wore it on the day the cameras went to Highgrove to work on the television programme about his parents.

The Princess, like any mother, is very particular about the two young Princes' appearance. She sometimes dresses them in matching blue and white outfits. Prince William is now old enough to have his own favourites. The red shorts he wore on his first day at school were particularly popular for a time. Prince William calls his mother 'Mummy' and his father 'Papa'. They call him William; the nickname 'Wills' seems to be less

Below and on pages 16 and 17: Both the Prince and Princess of Wales value enormously any free time they have to spend with their two young sons. Most of this free time is spent in the country at Highgrove.

popular now, though 'Wombat' seems to be on the increase. Prince Henry is just 'Harry'. Because of the enormous public interest in the children, their parents are extremely protective if anything goes wrong. When Prince Henry had a collision with a table at Highgrove this summer he ended up with some stitches above his nose. The staff were sworn to secrecy; even some of their own team back at Buckingham Palace did not know about it. In fact, it stayed secret until Prince Andrew's wedding day, when a close-up of the Buckingham Palace balcony showed the small scar left by the stitches as the Princess carried Prince Henry into public view for the first time since the accident.

Small bumps apart, Highgrove is a wonderful place for the royal children to grow up in. And there the Prince and Princess have a little more time to be on their own with their sons, and to play with them in the gardens and the farmland around the house.

On pages 18 and 19: The princes' uniforms were sent to Prince Charles, Colonel-in-Chief of the Parachute Regiment, as a Christmas present in 1985 from the families of '1 Para'. The uniforms were specially made from two full-sized ones which were cut down to fit. The stripes show that Prince William is a corporal and his younger brother a lance-corporal of the 1st Battalion of the Parachute Regiment. The berets were soaked and placed over pudding basins in an attempt to shrink them to fit the two small heads.

Facing page: Prince Henry holding the new pet rabbit, watched by his parents. The Princess herself used to keep small pets as a young child.
Below: Prince Charles is immensely proud of his wildflower meadow which borders the front drive of Highgrove.

Originally, when the Prince bought the house from the Macmillan family, the front of Highgrove could be seen from a public road. Now the ornamental gates, presented to the couple as a wedding present by the people of Tetbury, are as much as the passerby can see. Some strategically planted bushes and trees have given the family the chance to wander around knowing that no long lenses can be trained on them. In the early days, when the Prince was out for a walk or a ride in the grounds, he found photographers in the bushes.

When the Prince's Trust helped a young black photographer to start up in business, the Prince told him he did not want to see him at work down at Highgrove. It was not just a joke.

Though it is now difficult to see them, the Prince and Princess still have a wonderful view from the front of their house towards Tetbury. Between the trees, the spire and tower of Tetbury church stand silhouetted against the skyline. It is a favourite background for the Prince as he works on the wildflower garden which borders the driveway up to the front of the house.

The decision to keep the view clear of trees was made by a previous owner of the house, who actually paid £10,000 in 1891 to have the spire and tower restored. Highgrove was built at the end of the eighteenth century. In 1964 it was acquired by Maurice Macmillan, the Conservative MP and son of the former Prime Minister, Harold Macmillan,

Above and facing page: As well as the pet rabbit, the young princes have a small Shetland pony called Smokey. The Highgrove groom, Marion Cox is teaching them to ride and the Princess lends a hand whenever possible. Prince William is already a proficient rider for his age.

now the Earl of Stockton. He rarely lived there and it was offered for sale in 1980. It is said that Princess Anne, who lives only eight miles away at Gatcombe Park, pointed it out to the Prince of Wales.

He bought the freehold of the house and nearly 350 acres through the Duchy of Cornwall for what was said to be a sum of £800,000. Since then, much has been spent modernizing and brightening the inside, and landscaping outside. Like Kensington Palace, Highgrove House is smaller than might be expected for a royal residence. When it was advertised for sale in 1980 the estate agents called it 'a distinguished Georgian house with spacious but easily managed accommodation, comprising 4 Reception Rooms, Domestic Quarters, 9 Bedrooms, 6 Bath-

rooms, Nursery Wing, full central heating'.

That may have sounded large enough, but then the Prince was a bachelor. Now he has a wife and two children as well, and the attendant nannies, security and other back-up staff. Already, some staff who travel down from London have to stay in a local hotel, and it has been suggested that with the probable arrival of further children in future years, the house will not be large enough for a permanent royal home.

A new house, perhaps even purpose-built to the Prince's specifications, could be a solution. Clarence House, at present the home of Queen Elizabeth the Queen Mother, could be another, long-term, possibility.

In the early days of her marriage it was said that the Princess

Above and on pages 26 and 27: The family have become used to the sight of the red Wessex helicopters of the Queen's Flight arriving at Highgrove to collect the Prince and Princess for engagements. This time Prince Charles was on his way to visit Handsworth in Birmingham. Prince William knows exactly how to copy the signals given by the helicopter's signaller on the ground as the Wessex prepares to take off.

Facing page: The Princess of Wales carrying Prince Henry on her shoulders in the grounds of Highgrove

disliked Highgrove. If that were ever true, it is not now. She seems entirely happy relaxing in the gardens.

But, like many country houses, it is in the summer that Highgrove is at its best. Inside the house the polished wood floors reflect the work that has gone into them. Outside, the Prince's walled garden is in bloom, and there is the chance to use the swimming-pool. Prince William can play with his rabbit or go riding on his pony, Smokey.

The winter can sometimes be bleak, and occasionally fog can prevent the Queen's Flight helicopter landing or taking off. If this happens the Prince and Princess have to switch to cars to get to their engagements on time.

The blue support vehicle of the Queen's Flight is a regular sight in front of Highgrove. The family have got used to the red, royal helicopters landing where the horses were grazing only a few hours before.

The two young princes sometimes come out to wave goodbye to their mother or father as they go off to work by helicopter. Prince William has been in the support vehicle trying on the firefighter's helmet and he knows the name of the Prince's usual helicopter pilot, Commander Barry Kirby, RN. The Princess is always most careful not to let the children near the helicopter until the rotor blades have stopped. While it is on the ground, the children have had the chance to sit

in the pilot's and navigator's seats – as has the Princess herself.

During normal flights the royal travellers are in a self-contained compartment, unable to see into the cockpit. So, in July 1986, the Princess was given the chance to see what it is like up front. She climbed elegantly up the side into the cockpit, and, to her amusement, was presented with a special set of headphones covered in her fashion favourite of 1986, spots – each spot stuck on by the helicopter pilot. After being given an aerial view of the house and surrounding area, the Princess joked that she never knew there were so many swimming-pools in Tetbury.

But the real world stretches far beyond the swimming-pools. It is a world that demands patience, stamina, and application – and, greater even than these, sheer planning.

BEHIND THE SCENES

Organizing the lives of the Prince and Princess of Wales and making the whole operation run well is full-time work for about forty people. In addition, there are hundreds, perhaps even thousands, helping to make their engagements and foreign tours a success.

The head of their household is their Private Secretary. For six years the Prince's Private Secretary was Edward Adeane, son of a former Private Secretary to the Queen and a man known for his remarkable memory for detail. This parting of the ways was accompanied by reports of disagreements with the Princess. It may be that the very fact that Mr Adeane did not wait for his successor to be appointed tells its own story.

It meant that David Roycroft, thirty-eight, a Foreign Office man on a three-year secondment to the Prince and Princess of Wales' Office, was thrown in at the deep end. In his role as Assistant Private Secretary, he would normally attend to the day-to-day planning of the royal diary. But for nine months he had to handle other issues as well.

By then Sir John Riddell, fifty-two years old, had been appointed the new Private Secretary. Naturally, there was speculation that it had been a difficult job to fill. Sir John's title is hereditary; he is the thirteenth baronet in a line reaching back as far as 1628. But he had had no experience in royal circles. Formerly a banker and Deputy Chairman of the Independent Broadcasting

On page 34: Every year thousands of letters arrive at the Prince of Wales' Office at Buckingham Palace from all over the world.

On page 35: Organizing the lives of the Prince and Princess of Wales and making the whole operation run smoothly is full-time work for about forty people. On overseas tours members of the Household accompany the Prince and Princess to coordinate arrangements, do the necessary clerical work and stay in touch with Buckingham Palace at home. On the trip to Japan in May 1986 the party comprised: (Front row, from left to right) Surgeon Commander Ian Jenkins (Medical Officer to Their Royal Highnesses), David Roycroft (Assistant Private Secretary), Miss Anne Beckwith-Smith (Lady-in-Waiting), the Prince and Princess of Wales, Sir John Riddell (Private Secretary), Lieutenant-Colonel Brian Anderson (Equerry to the Prince) and Victor Chapman (Press Secretary). (Back row) Sergeant Ron Lewis (Baggage Master), Michael Fawcett (Valet), Superintendent Colin Trimming (the Prince's Protection Officer), Miss Helen Rowe (Lady Clerk to the Assistant Private Secretary), Miss Fay Marshalsea (Dresser), Miss Julia Tingey (Lady Clerk to the Private Secretary), Miss Evelyn Dagley (Dresser), Miss Kiloran McGrigor (Lady Clerk to the Press Secretary), Inspector Graham Smith (the Princess's Protection Officer), Harold Brown (Butler), the Hon. Rupert Fairfax (Assistant Private Secretary for Industrial Affairs), and Richard Dalton (Hairdresser).

David Roycroft, Assistant Private Secretary to the Prince of Wales, in his office at Buckingham Palace. On loan from the Foreign Office he completed his three-year secondment in August 1986. His main task was the day-to-day planning of the royal diary.

Authority, he had stood, unsuccessfully, as a Conservative candidate at two elections.

He eased himself carefully into the job, spending his first royal tour – of Australia and the United States – seeing the way things were done. He left much of the detailed tour work to Roycroft, who had done all the advance planning. When he said to journalists on tour that he had not realized quite how much the job involved he was not entirely joking.

Now he combines the roles of policy adviser and confidante to the royal couple, ceremonial figurehead of the household, and supervisor of the detailed planning of the royal engagements.

Under him is a new Deputy Private Secretary, Mr Humphrey Mews, a former army officer who, unlike his predecessors in the job, is a permanent appointment rather than on a secondment. This may be in response to complaints that the couple's staff rotate or change so often that there is a lack of continuity. Only

two of the present royal household have been in their jobs longer than a year.

The fastest rotation is among the equerries. Traditionally, one officer from the Services worked two years for the Prince and one year for the Princess. Now, a third equerry has been brought in to help, Captain Alison Ewan, aged twenty-nine, of the Women's Royal Army Corps – the first woman appointed to this post. She helps to organize the details of engagements with Lieutenant-Colonel Brian Anderson, the Prince's Equerry, and Lieutenant-Commander Richard Aylard does the same job for the Princess. But there is enough flexibility for the army officer to help with the Princess's army engagements and the lieutenant-commander to lend a hand when the Prince is visiting the navy.

To do their jobs properly the senior people in the household have to show great understanding towards the people they are working for, and about the pressures, the strains and the many

frustrations they have to endure.

It is, in fact, the people in the real front-line who have stayed longest. Miss Anne Beckwith-Smith has been lady-in-waiting to the Princess since 1981. A lady-in-waiting can just help out at engagements by, say, collecting the flowers presented to the Princess. Miss Beckwith-Smith does this and very much more. The Private Secretary and his Deputy naturally work for both the Prince and Princess but neither would dispute that it is she who is the Princess's closest adviser and friend. Deeply loyal to her employer, nobody has a better idea of what the Princess would like and dislike, would want to do and would not want to do. There are now five other ladies-in-waiting to help in attendance at engagements, while Anne Beckwith-Smith works more in her office at Buckingham Palace and visits the Princess at Kensington Palace.

Above left: Captain Alison Ewan is the Prince's Assistant Equerry.
Above right: Lieutenant-Commander Richard Aylard, a naval officer, is Equerry to the Princess of Wales.

Below: The Princess of Wales with Miss Anne Beckwith-Smith during a programme meeting at Kensington Palace and on a visit to Belfast in October 1985. Miss Beckwith-Smith is the Princess's senior lady-in-waiting of a total number of six who help at engagements.

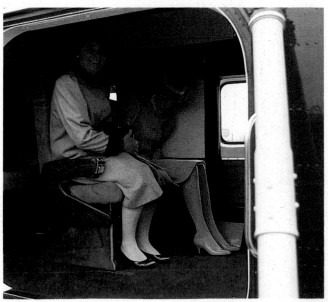

Right: The Princess of Wales visiting the John Radcliffe Hospital in Oxford in January 1986. When she carries out engagements by herself in Britain the Princess is usually accompanied by (from left to right) a royal protection officer (here, Inspector Graham Smith), her Equerry, Lieutenant-Commander Richard Aylard, and a lady-in-waiting (here, Miss Anne Beckwith-Smith). The Princess is received by the Lord Lieutenant of Oxfordshire, Sir Ashley Ponsonby, Bt. MC (right). One of the duties of a lord lieutenant is to escort members of the royal family when they visit his county.

On pages 38 and 39: While the Prince of Wales met members of the 'UK-Japan 2000 Group' at the Akasaka Palace in Tokyo in May 1986, his Private Secretary, Sir John Riddell (second left) and Assistant Private Secretary, David Roycroft (left) conversed quietly in a corner.

The next closest in line to the Prince and Princess are the royal protection officers. They probably spend more time with them than anybody else. On a drive down to Highgrove or flight to Scotland, the detectives are always close by.

Superintendent Colin Trimming is the Prince's senior detective and runs the unit. Inspector Graham Smith is the number two and the Princess's protection officer. To keep 24-hour security the work is shared with Inspector Tony Parker, Inspector Allan Peters and other officers.

The detectives have to dress and act as courtiers but also always have to remember that their job is royal safety. Some colleagues in the police force suspect that royal detectives come to think of themselves as courtiers first and policemen second, but there is no evidence at all that the undoubted team spirit within the royal household and staff has diminished the policemen's efficiency. In keeping with British police tradition, the de-tectives conceal their guns; they have never been seen to pull them out in public.

Again, the security around Kensington Palace and Highgrove may appear low key but nobody should make the mistake of thinking that it is lax. For instance, at Highgrove the main police surveillance point is completely screened, but if you cannot see them they can certainly see you. There is a bank of television monitors showing any movement around the grounds and there are many other alarm systems. Anybody who tried to rush in and make mischief at Highgrove or Kensington Palace would find a back-up system they had not expected.

On foreign tours, the detectives work in co-operation with security forces such as the State Department Security in the United States and the Federal Police force in Australia. These forces try to provide people the royal party have got to know on previous occasions. In the United States it is a black detective called

'T.J.' Mallory; in Australia it is a Scotsman long resident in Canberra, George Davidson.

There is sometimes a variety of police forces. When the Prince and Princess visited a shopping centre outside Washington in 1985, there were four different police uniforms on display: the plain clothes State Department security men, the local police, the local Highway Patrol and the store's own security men and women. Amid this gathering of walkie-talkies and earpieces, the decision to go ahead with a walk-about and when to finish it was made by the Prince's man, Colin Trimming. At the end, he could be clearly seen politely gesturing to his royal employers to get back in their car. The policemen normally refer to the Prince as 'the boss'. This time it was the policeman who was in charge.

Just about the only part of a royal engagement with which the detectives are not involved is the initial decision-making process about which events the royal couple will attend. Every year thousands of letters arrive at the

On overseas tours it is the responsibility of the host country to provide security in liaison with Their Royal Highnesses' royal protection officers.

The many thousands of letters and invitations addressed to the Prince and Princess that arrive each year in Their Royal Highnesses' Office are read and sifted by the lady clerks.

Prince of Wales' Office in Buckingham Palace. Among them are invitations for the Prince and Princess to go to events ranging from the first night of an opera to a child's birthday party.

When the office staff first sift through these invitations they are looking to see which are from charities, trusts and causes that the Prince or Princess are particularly interested in, which are from parts of the country they want to visit or already plan to visit, and which fit into a royal timetable which already has portions blocked off for important events such as a state visit, and for such traditional royal holidays as Christmas at Windsor, the New Year at Sandringham and August in Scotland.

Those which are passed on after this process are first presented as a draft diary to the Prince. Those he approves are then put before a programme meeting held twice a year in the dining-room at Kensington Palace. Round the table are represented all aspects of the Prince's life – from policy to polo, from the Duchy of Cornwall to the press. Sir John Riddell may sit next to the Prince's polo manager, Major Ronald Ferguson. And Prince William sometimes pops in on his way to nursery school.

The aims of the meeting are to check that there is no clash between the proposed arrangements and any other plans, and to see which of the Prince's engagements the Princess plans to attend

as well. This process has its lighter moments. In December 1985 the Prince was invited to a reception at the Royal College of Music, of whose centenary appeal he is President. When the Princess, President of the friendly rival – the Royal Academy of Music – said that she would like to come as well, the Prince could not resist a smile and a gentle dig in the ribs.

The Princess consults Anne Beckwith-Smith and they take notes so that afterwards, when they know which dates are still free, they can begin filling the Princess's diary of engagements.

The decisions taken at the programme meeting are not final. There is still time afterwards to fit in a last-minute event, provided that the will, and time, are there.

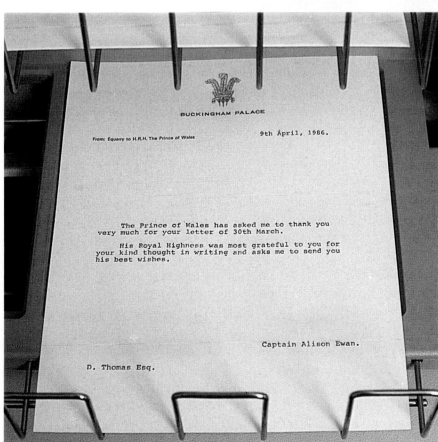

Their Royal Highnesses' Office is now fully computerized. Letters and the Prince and Princess's speeches are prepared on word processors. Captain Alison Ewan deals with many of the replies.

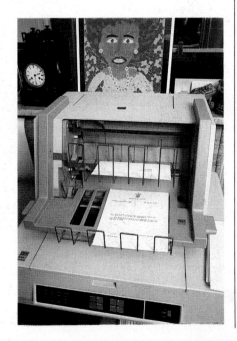

Once an engagement has been decided the organizers are informed and a date is fixed for a 'recce', a reconnoitre of the event. This is done by the Private Secretary, his Assistant, an equerry or, for some of the Princess's events, Anne Beckwith-Smith. They are usually accompanied by the detective who will be at the engagement on the day, and if there is expected to be particular press interest, their Press Secretary, Victor Chapman, may go along too.

On a 'recce' the royal representative wants to hear what the local organizer of the event has in mind and he can advise on protocol and practical issues. How much the Palace representative has to do depends on the experience of the local organizer.

Sometimes the issues can be decided by only three or four people. Sometimes an equerry will turn up to find more than ten people, representing everybody from the local lord lieutenant to the parish council, from the chief constable to the local bobby.

When the royal representative returns to the Palace he or she has the details entered on a computerized diary so that at any stage anybody in the office can call up the system and find out who is organizing what at which event. The computers and word processors in the office were installed during 1985 and 1986. Before that, with all the mass of paper work, the office could at times resemble that of an over-worked barrister.

Overseas tours inevitably take a great deal of organization. So far the Prince and Princess have paid two official visits to Australia and Canada, and they have

Above: A 'recce' held in Fiji on the way to Australia in October 1985. Discussing arrangements with two Fijian officials for the formal visit to be made on the return journey are the Assistant Private Secretary, David Roycroft and the Press Secretary, Victor Chapman.
Facing page above: After a 'recce' has been carried out details of the arrangements for an engagement are entered on a computerized diary.
Facing page below: The result of the advance planning – the Prince and Princess's one-hour official visit to Fiji.

On pages 44 and 45: A programme meeting at Kensington Palace. Among the many who attend are (from left to right): David Roycroft, Miss Anne Beckwith-Smith, the Princess and Prince, Sir John Riddell, and Major Ronald Ferguson, the Prince's polo manager who ensures that the Prince's match schedule fits in with other commitments.

been also to the United States, Austria, Italy and Japan. The least known of their official visits was the hour they spent on the tarmac at Fiji airport in November 1985, being entertained by local dancers while their airplane was refuelled en route from Australia to the United States.

These overseas visits are sometimes more complex because there are so many different bodies to deal with. Although many Commonwealth countries are very experienced in organizing royal tours there are often local tensions between federal, state and city authorities.

The Prince and Princess of Wales at a reception for media during their visit to Japan in May 1986. The media receptions are an important fixture on the overseas tours and a rare opportunity for local and travelling media to meet the royal family informally.

A visit to Australia almost always involves a visit to the capital, Canberra, to satisfy the Federal Government. And in some countries the Palace team must be careful that local officials do not overload the visit with too many engagements to keep the different authorities happy.

Australia and Canada both provide experienced Tour Direc-tors, and much of the detailed planning is negotiated with them. They are rewarded with some personal memento from the visitors, such as one of the photo-graphs which the Prince and Princess often sign on the flight out to an overseas tour.

If the tour is to a country the royal couple have not visited before there is, inevitably, more work to be done. The 'recce' is normally conducted by the Private Secretary or the Assistant Private Secretary or both, along with the Press Secretary and a detective. One of the Press Secre-tary's main problems will be striking a happy balance between the demands of the local news media, those of the press corps which always travels out from Britain for such tours and those of the local security authorities.

The needs of the media are in-variably in the minds of the organizers of the tours. There is no point holding an official visit if it cannot be photographed and re-ported widely on television, radio and in the newspapers. So there has to be a balance between events which have a formal signi-ficance and those which will make a good picture.

On the 'recce' the Palace team will want to know every detail of what is expected of the royal couple, and will be asked for advice on how they should be addressed (as Their Royal High-nesses, Sir or Ma'am) and how they should be greeted (curtsying and bowing are not compulsory).

They will be asked what kind of food the Prince and Princess like (they do not take their own chefs on these tours) and what

kind of drink they like (wine is acceptable). The local organizers will be reminded also that great care must be taken not to allow the press to photograph the Prince and Princess eating or drinking.

The timetable will be agreed down to every last detail so that the 'recce' team can return with all the necessary information for everybody going on the tour: that is, from the royal visitors downwards.

Advance preparations for overseas tours include details about what the Prince and Princess will eat and drink. The Japan visit included an ancient tea ceremony, a banquet with the imperial family and a traditional dinner seated on the floor.

In preparation for the Gulf Tour in November 1986 the Princess had a series of meetings in August at Kensington Palace with dress designers, David and Elizabeth Emanuel. As she told them: 'It's a difficult one, this tour, because I have to hide my elbows, and have threequarter-length hemlines. I think we might avoid the spots too!

'The tour is ten days to two weeks and we might be changing two or three times a day; it's a bit testing on the wardrobe. But I don't have to wear too many hats, so that's a relief.'

On pages 52 and 53: At Government House, Melbourne Miss Evelyn Dagley, one of the Princess's dressers, prepares the outfit the Princess has chosen to wear that day to go to church and to visit the Royal Botanic Gardens. On tour the dresser's job is hectic and there are often several changes of clothes in one day.

51

The Prince will need to know where he is scheduled to make a speech, what the issues in the country are, what the hosts would like to hear – and what they would not like to hear. He and the Princess will need to know what the weather will be like so that they can choose the right clothes. The Princess, in particular, will need to know if there are any traditions about forms of dress that she should observe. For example, visiting the Arabs means some delicate decisions by the Princess. Is it necessary to wear long dresses or skirts to avoid upsetting Moslem custom? For the Gulf Tour in November 1986 the Princess had a series of meetings in her sitting-room in Kensington Palace with her advisers and dress designers on her outfits. Their many designs were laid out on the carpet in the search for something that would help to promote British fashion but not at the expense of local feelings.

In the preparations for any foreign tour her dressers, Evelyn Dagley and Fay Marshalsea, are crucial in helping to work out how many suitcases will be needed and when and where.

The Prince's valets, Ken Stronach and Michael Fawcett, will be doing the same for him.

Last-minute preparations for the Royal Tour of Australia and the visit to Washington in October 1985. At Kensington Palace the Prince and Princess's butler, Mr Harold Brown packs the personal stationery to be used on the overseas tour, ready to be taken to Heathrow Airport. In the evening he and other members of the Household are taken to the airport by coach.

They will then tell Sergeant Ron Lewis of the Welsh Guards, the Prince and Princess's baggage master. He will need to work out how to move the luggage from place to place, who will collect it at the airport, how much will be moved into the official residence and unpacked, and how much is left packed for the next stop.

Only then is the royal road show ready to roll.

In 1985 and 1986 the mobile computerized office arrived. On royal tours the household have always set up shop somewhere, normally in an hotel room, to co-ordinate arrangements, do the necessary clerical work, and stay in touch with Buckingham

Palace. Two or three secretaries, called lady clerks, are taken along to work in this office. Word processors are now taken on the road, and not the old typewriters. In Texas, for instance, the Prince's speeches were taken out, both in the original longhand in which he wrote them and on floppy discs so that changes could be put in up until the last minute.

Also in the mobile office is a fax machine which can send documents to and from Buckingham Palace. It is also used to send the tour party important extracts from the day's London newspapers. The newspapers themselves arrive from London on the next airplane out, along with any highly confidential documents for the Prince which are not sent on the fax machine.

With the experience of many past tours the household attends to every detail. There is special writing paper headed 'The Royal Party on Tour', on which the thank-you letters are typed. Sergeant Lewis has his boxes for the royal standards which are taken from city to city for the official cars.

Above: On overseas tours most of the Household stay in a hotel near the Prince and Princess of Wales. Here, the staff set up the mobile office which now includes a fax machine. This enables the royal party to stay in touch with Buckingham Palace when on tour.

Below: Everything is meticulously labelled for its final destination.

In a fast-moving tour from city to city some of the greatest stress is on the valets and dressers. They sometimes spend most of the night packing and unpacking, and when the royal party board the airplanes there is sometimes a last-minute scramble. While the Prince and Princess were getting comfortably into their seats on the RAF VC10 at Palm Beach airport in November, the valet and dresser were running up and down the back steps, their arms full of boxes and cases.

But perhaps the most frantic stopover of the year was during the flight on Concorde from London to Austria. The Princess boarded the flight at Heathrow and Concorde then flew to northern Italy in order to collect

the Prince, who had been on a private holiday, sketching.

In order to minimize the hold-up to the fare-paying passengers on board, the stop in Milan was a 'racing' one, with Concorde's engines left running, and no time to open the baggage hold. First up the steps was one of the Prince's valets, Michael Fawcett, almost brimming over with the gifts and souvenirs the Prince had been given. And he was not far behind, his left arm in a sling after his gardening accident and wearing ear defenders against the noise of Concorde's engines.

It was not the most elegant of royal departures, but the speed of it all enabled Concorde to arrive in Austria on time, flying the flag for British Week in Vienna.

PRINCE OF WALES OFFICE

Above left: Sergeant Ron Lewis, the baggage master, loading the Prince's polo sticks on board.
Above right: Loading the Princess's wardrobe on to the airplane.
Left: The mobile office packed ready for its next destination.

Facing page: The luggage waiting at Canberra airport to be loaded on to the Royal Australian Air Force Boeing 707 for the early morning flight to Washington via Fiji and Honolulu.
On pages 58 and 59: The Prince and Princess of Wales on the tarmac at Heathrow Airport with the flight and cabin crew of Concorde after their return journey from Vienna in April 1986.

ROYAL TOURS

Anybody arriving at Fiji airport at dawn one morning in October 1985 would have been surprised to find the heir to the British throne in casual clothes, pacing up and down the runway stretching his legs after a 23-hour flight from London, and his wife in a slightly crumpled blouse and skirt standing at the top of the steps rubbing the sleep out of her eyes.

This was perhaps the most casual royal arrival at any airport. The reason was that this stay in Fiji was purely a refueling stop on the way to the royal tour of Australia.

The Royal Australian Air Force, who flew the jet for the flight from London to Melbourne, asked the Palace if – for logistical reasons – the royal couple would mind going the 'wrong way round' over North America, rather than the Indian Ocean. It added a number of hours to the flight and therefore made it even more essential for the Prince and Princess to stretch their legs at Fiji.

After the Prince returned to the plane, the Princess walked down to the tarmac to chat with her staff. The Governor-General of Fiji, hearing that she was there, could not miss the opportunity to check with her that the arrangements were satisfactory for the one-hour official visit the couple were due to make on their way back from Australia. Being a proper Governor-General he was wearing a traditional Fijian outfit, which is how it came about that the Princess and he stood on an airport tarmac wearing skirts of exactly the same length.

Above: The Prince of Wales stretching his legs on the edge of the runway of Fiji airport on the way to Australia for the Royal Tour in October 1985.
Left: While the Prince was taking his early morning walk the Princess talked to his valet, Ken Stronach on the rear steps of the Royal Australian Air Force Boeing 707.

Back on the aircraft for the next part of the flight down to Melbourne there was a surprise for Ken Stronach, the most experienced of the Prince's two valets. The Royal Australian Air Force cabin crew produced a birthday cake and everybody joined in the airborne birthday party. As

Stronach blushed at the fuss, the Princess joked with him that for once it was the behind-the-scenes staff, not her, who were embarrassed by all the attention. She agreed with the message on the cake 'God Bless You', but revealed to Ken that it had been stored by 'the loo' for 24 hours.

On page 60: The Princess of Wales talking to the Governor-General of Fiji during the official one-hour visit which the royal couple made on their return journey from Australia.
On page 61: The Princess of Wales was less formally dressed when she met the Governor-General on the outward journey to Australia. On this occasion the stop-over in Fiji was for re-fuelling and a reconnoitre for the return visit.
Right: Shortly after the stop-over in Fiji a surprise birthday cake was produced for the Prince of Wales' valet, Ken Stronach.

The royal couple came out from their private compartment to join in the in-flight surprise birthday party which had been organized at Their Royal Highnesses' suggestion.

As the cake was cut into pieces for the royal entourage and the champagne was passed round, the Prince and Princess talked with their staff about the length of the flight and the tour ahead. On the approach to Melbourne the final touches were put to the organization. The detailed plans for the days ahead were checked for the last time and the Prince's Australian equerry polished the ceremonial sword to be carried at official functions.

Thirty-three hours out of London the airplane touched down in Melbourne. For most of the flight the Prince and Princess had been in a separate compartment from the rest of the passengers. The only visitors up front were when their butler, valet or dresser were needed or when senior staff were invited up to have lunch or dinner.

Once the airplane had landed all those who would follow the Prince and Princess down the steps began to file into the royal compartment. But nobody disembarked until the Australian pest-control officer had walked the length of the aircraft spraying royals and commoners alike.

The Princess was keen to leave the aircraft after the long flight and get the tour under way. 'Let's go', she said, making a gesture with her arms of a locomotive getting up steam. The Prince, who has been visiting Australia since he was at school at Melbourne's Geelong Grammar, just stayed in his seat until the official 'off'. After a thank-you to the crew, the Princess reminded the Prince, as if he needed to be told, 'you go first'. They walked down the steps into the spring sunshine of Australia and the visit had begun.

After a very long flight such as this one the royal planners always allow the Prince and Princess a few hours to sleep off the effects. But it is probably a lot less time than most people need to recover fully from the jet lag.

The Prince and Princess of Wales share a last-minute joke with their Household on arrival at Melbourne airport

Facing page: The ten-day Royal Tour of Australia in October 1985 was a busy one. Among the many engagements was a visit to the Alcoa aluminium smelter in Portland, Victoria where all the visitors, including the Princess, had to wear protective goggles and helmet.

Asked about what it is that attracts him to Australia, the Prince says:

'It's partly because, of course, I was there at school for six months and it's the only country I have ever spent that long in; so, inevitably, it is a sort of second home in that sense. I've always had an affection for it because the Australians were so kind to me when I was there in 1966, and made it much easier for me, being a somewhat shy and awkward youth. It certainly brought me out because they're very forthright and forthcoming.

'And also because I think the country is a great country, with immense potential. It's a big country with every kind of conceivable variety from one end to the other and one side to the other – different climates, different opportunities and so on. And I enjoy the Australian people, they make me laugh and I like the directness because it means you

Right: The Princess of Wales always loves an opportunity of talking to children. After church at St Paul's Cathedral in Melbourne, she and the Prince toured the Royal Botanic Gardens and chatted to several groups of onlookers.

Facing page: The Princess of Wales talking to children in Macedon, Victoria. The Prince and Princess saw the rehabilitation of the small township which was the scene of devastating bush fires in 1983, when over one hundred people died.

Below: On the last afternoon in Victoria the Prince and Princess of Wales attended the Melbourne Cup races at Flemington racecourse. Melbourne Cup Day is the highlight in the Victorian racing and social calendar.
On page 73: The Princess of Wales at the State Dinner held at Government House, Melbourne on the last evening of their stay in Victoria. The Princess is wearing a favourite blue velvet and lace evening dress, diamond and sapphire jewellery and her Spencer tiara.

can be direct back again. I always enjoy seeing Australians in Australia or over here or anywhere in the world; and New Zealanders, too, for that matter.'

The first event on this tour was a reception for the news media at Government House, which is the official residence of the Governor-General of the State of Victoria. The Prince and Princess were based there during their ten-day visit to celebrate the 150th anniversary of the foundation of Victoria.

Media receptions are curious events, a hangover from the days when those covering a royal tour were made to feel part of the official party. Nowadays, it is a rare chance for a face-to-face meeting between the Prince and

Princess and the specialist royal correspondents from Fleet Street.

All those attending the receptions are reminded of the strict rule that nothing which is said by the Prince and Princess can be reported. In this atmosphere the Princess sometimes teases or complains to reporters about things they have reported about her. The Prince plays a fairly straight bat, depending on the firm handshake, the wry smile and a direct look in the eyes.

In the past all this has temporarily flattered the media into believing the royals do not think quite so badly of them, and has reminded the royal side that there are human beings amid the battery of cameras and notebooks facing them. However, the

Melbourne media reception was a turning point. A group of Fleet Street reporters was anxious to find out about reports that the Prince had told Mr Rod Hackney, an adviser on architecture, that he did not want to be King of a country divided into 'haves' and 'have-nots', which was taken to be a worry about the inner city riots in Britain that summer.

The morning after this reception the newspapers reported the Prince telling aides that he had felt betrayed by Hackney and that he never used the phrase 'When I become King' because 'it was so pompous'. The Prince's Press Secretary was annoyed that the papers had broken the tradition of not reporting receptions. The reporters claimed that they had had some official clearance.

Since then the invitations for the media receptions have never been quite the same. The tendency is to favour the media resident in the country being visited; that is, local newspapers and broadcasters and the local correspondents and staff of the British media. The press corps that has travelled out from London now gets less opportunity to meet the couple it spends so much time writing about.

There seem to be, now and again, prickly relations between Buckingham Palace and Fleet Street. The reporters from the popular press say part of the problem is that often there is no 'story' in the traditional journalistic sense. Particularly on foreign tours, when there is considerable cost for a newspaper in sending a photographer and reporter and the expectation of a story each day, the reporter is sometimes little more than a caption writer for the words below the photograph of the Princess's latest outfit. So the photographers work, or hunt, together as a group, and the reporters form a separate group. Sometimes, there is more bad feeling between a reporter and photographer from the same newspaper, than between rival photographers or reporters.

Whenever any members of the royal family make their dislike of the news media public, Fleet Street's reply is that the royals would soon start worrying if nothing about them appeared in the papers. Some of them say that the problem on the royal side is that it is not always appreciated what it takes to get a good picture. Sometimes it is an unexpected moment in an unlikely setting that produces the best picture, and that is why there are often so many photographers and cameramen rushing around – and sometimes why so little is used.

A good example was the visit by the Prince and Princess to an aluminium smelter in the Australian town of Portland. The reason for the visit was quite simply that the Victorian Government wanted to give a royal blessing to what had been a very expensive scheme. When the visit appeared in the royal schedule the media yawned. But all the press corps duly turned up and captured the moment when the Princess could not contain her giggles at the sight of the Prince in a white protective helmet that was a few sizes too big for him.

On the airplane back to Melbourne the press was well pleased. It had been a good day, there were good pictures and a good story. The Victorian Government had got the publicity for their smelter and the royals had had a little fun. The only people who might have felt put out were some of the smelter workers who, trying to publicize their grievances, had refused to show the royals how part of the plant worked. Compared with the royal giggles, that was a non-story and sunk without trace.

Another attempt by a union to use the royal visit to its advantage came unstuck in Canberra when the royal couple visited the site of the new Australian Federal Parliament. The workers there belong to Australia's most militant union, the Australian Building Construction Employees and Builders', Labourers' Federation, whose leader has spent periods in jail. As the royal party approached the site, they caught sight of union banners – and the 'Eureka' flag which is the union's symbol. But for all the effort the union had made to put its point, once the members met the royal couple face to face they could not have been friendlier. There were wolf whistles for the Princess, and three cheers for her and the Prince.

After touring the site, the Princess stood and chatted with a labourer who had taken off his T-shirt and tied it round his head. It was not the way most people would dress to meet royalty, but it said a lot about the way in which a potentially uneasy encounter had been defused.

It was the unexpected fashion notes that livened up the press coverage of the Australian tour. The Princess surprised everybody by turning up at a charity ball with an emerald necklace, a wedding gift from the Queen, as a headband. The press reports said it was because of sunburn on her neck. Nobody asked where was the tiara which she had been due to wear. The official description of the outfit has the line about the tiara crossed out.

Facing page: In Canberra the Princess of Wales delighted the construction workers when she and the Prince visited the site of the new Australian Federal Parliament which is due to be completed in 1988.

Below: The Princess of Wales looking stylish in a black and white outfit for Melbourne Cup Day. The sweeping shawl collar was fastened at the hip with large black buttons.

Nobody asked whether the tiara could not be found that evening in all the packing and repacking that goes on during a tour.

The headband intrigued the Australian fashion writers much more than their usual annual talking-point, the outfits on Melbourne Cup Day. This is the highlight of the Victorian racing and social calendar.

The royal couple allowed television cameras to follow them throughout the day to give viewers an idea of a royal day 'on the road'. At Government House they wake early. At home, the Prince sometimes listens to the farming programme on the radio, which starts at 6.10 am. On tour, waking-up time depends on the timetable for the day. Whether at home or on tour, breakfast is prepared by the butler, Harold Brown. His tray of cereals, tea and a flower is the same wherever they go. For the Princess further continuity comes from her hairdresser, Richard Dalton. He is an early arrival at Government House and the time the Princess spends having her hair done is also a chance to chat before the official work ahead.

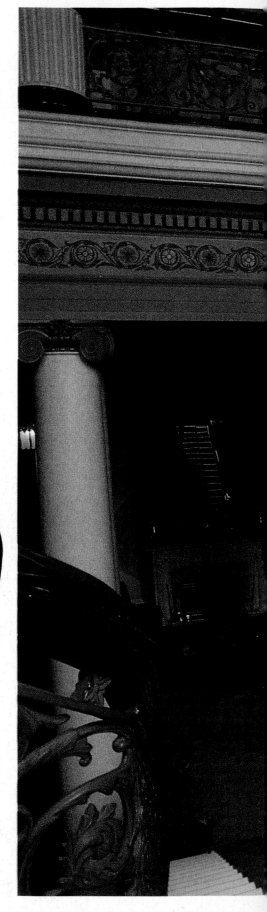

At Kensington Palace, several newspapers are delivered: some from the serious end of the range, some from the middle. On tour, extracts from the London papers are sent over on a fax machine; the real newspapers follow by air later, but there is not always time to read them.

On Melbourne Cup Day, some Australians dress up, and some dress down. The royal visitors followed the tradition of morning dress for the men and smart outfits for the ladies.

So, down the corridor from the royal suite in Government House, the Prince's morning suit was being brushed by his valet, Ken Stronach, and the Princess's outfit was being prepared by Evelyn Dagley.

As the household gathered at the foot of the staircase, the Prince could not resist a word about the smell of mothballs and the good business being done by Moss Bros, the London hire firm.

Their hostess at Government House, Lady Young, the wife of the Lieutenant-Governor, had organized the traditional Melbourne Cup buttonhole of yellow roses for the party. But the Prince had already decided on a blue flower he had seen in a bowl in his suite. 'I like being different', he told her.

The Prince and Princess of Wales' Household on tour in Canberra, November 1985. (Front row from left to right) Victor Chapman (Press Secretary), David Roycroft (Assistant Private Secretary), Mrs George West (Lady-in-Waiting), the Prince and Princess of Wales, Duncan Anderson (the Australian Commonwealth Director of the Royal Tour), Sir John Riddell (Private Secretary), and Major Ronald Ferguson (polo manager). (Middle row) Commander Brian Robertson (the Australian Equerry to His Royal Highness for the Royal Tour), Miss Kiloran McGrigor (Lady Clerk to the Press Secretary), Miss Emma Fenn-Smith (Lady Clerk to the Assistant Private Secretary), Miss Julia Tingey (Lady Clerk to the Private Secretary), Miss Fay Marshalsea (Dresser), Miss Evelyn Dagley (Dresser), Surgeon Commander Ian Jenkins (Medical Officer), and Detective Inspector George Davidson (Australian Protection Officer). (Back row) Richard Dalton (Hairdresser), Harold Brown (Butler), Inspector Tony Parker (the Prince's Protection Officer), Inspector Graham Smith (the Princess's Protection Officer), Ken Stronach (Valet) and Sergeant Ron Lewis (Baggage Master).

Those waiting at the course were not as interested in the Prince's buttonhole as in his wife's choice of clothes. The photographers with long lenses caught first sight of her in the open carriage procession down the course. 'Oh, no,' went up the cry, 'it's the black and white one she's worn before.' And immediately the story was decided. The Princess had snubbed Australian fashion by wearing an old outfit. If she had worn something new she might equally have been told she was extravagant.

All over Australia people organize sweepstakes on the Melbourne Cup, and there was one in the royal household too. So, although the Prince and Princess did not bet on the race, they had horses to follow. They found both their horses were soon out of the running, but the horse drawn for Prince William was just beaten into second place.

Returning to Government House, the Princess confessed to Lady Young that her horse was last, but one of the royal detectives, Inspector Tony Parker, was able to say that he had picked the winner. 'You can take us all out to dinner,' the Princess said.

In fact, dinner had already been arranged. It was for the notables of the State of Victoria in the dining-room of Government House. All went smoothly that evening until a small, unexpected hitch on the way up to bed. After saying good night the Princess caught her tiara on her dress and had to stop on the staircase and untangle it. The moment was shared with the ten people at the bottom of the stairs, and a few million watching on television a year later.

On arriving at Fiji airport for the short official visit in November 1985 the Prince of Wales inspected the guard of honour. The colourful Fijian soldiers in their scarlet and white uniforms are reputed to be the most precisely drilled soldiers in the world.

After the short welcoming ceremony the Princess of Wales talked to the local dancers who had just performed in front of the royal visitors.

It was also a year later before another part of that royal tour was shown to the public. On their way from Australia to Washington, the Prince and Princess did, indeed, spend the time while their plane was re-fuelled in Fiji being entertained by the Fijian Government. It was probably the shortest official visit anywhere – one hour in a speci-ally built native pavilion on the tarmac at the airport.

The crowd sang 'Happy Birth-day' to the Prince, even though it was a week before the actual date. Local dancers, some of them rather overweight, performed and then fell at the feet of the royal visitors in a symbolic wel-come. The Prince drank tea and the entourage was served large,

exotic fruit juices. The whole occasion was over in under the hour and some said this was an excellent form of royal visit. Enough local colour and charm to fill two days of a normal tour and all done with the convenience and security provided by an air-port tarmac.

The press corps had gone on ahead to Honolulu, where the couple were to spend a night before flying to Washington. This had prompted absurd head-lines of a 'Hawaiian love-nest'. But anybody who has ever spent a night in an airport hotel be-tween flights could have pre-dicted it would be a lot less glamorous than that. The photo-graphers were keen to get a photograph that said the royals

Facing page: Perfect autumn weather greeted the royal couple on the first day of their stay in Washington in November 1985. Before lunch the Prince and Princess planted a tree in the garden of the British Residence to commemorate their visit.

Below: A quiet lunch at the British Residence in Washington on the first day of the Prince and Princess's visit. During lunch the Ambassador, Sir Oliver Wright went through the details of the programme with the royal party.
On pages 86 and 87: One of the Princess of Wales' concerns is the growing worldwide problem of drug addiction. During the stay in Washington she accompanied Mrs Nancy Reagan on a visit to the drug rehabilitation programme, 'Straight', in Springfield, Virginia.

were in Hawaii. It was decided that photographs of Hawaii must have beaches and palm trees in them, so negotiations were held with the royal party.

The Prince and Princess agreed to one of the things they like least, standing in a posed position for a photograph. Unfortunately, local law meant the beach could not be closed to the public, and as the Prince and Princess posed in front of their hotel, the idyllic scene was spoilt by sightseers gawping behind them. It was a pretty rotten picture and hardly anybody used it. Much happier were those who had caught the Prince going for a quick swim earlier and watched as his rather baggy trunks were nearly swept down by the surf.

Ahead in Washington lay an even more demanding media. The build-up by the American magazines and newspapers was unprecedented. *Life* magazine carried pages and pages of photographs on the eve of the tour. Odd that, despite this, and all the photographers *Life* had covering the tour, not a single picture of the actual visit appeared in the next edition.

Maybe the American media expected too much. Maybe it was the enormous security that prevented the royal party meeting any ordinary Americans in walkabouts until the last day in Washington. Maybe they simply forgot that the Prince and Princess are ordinary human beings and expected them to walk on water.

THE KID
STRAI
WELCOME OUR
THE FIRST
AND
THE PRINCESS
ESERVED

There were some good 'stories': the Princess's hat nearly being blown away by the wind and President Reagan calling her 'Princess David'. But, ironically, for all the coverage and the American tradition of open access for the media, some of the most interesting things happened out of public view. The Princess's dance with John Travolta was photographed by a White House cameraman but the picture has never been officially released.

The climax of the 'mediafest' came in Palm Beach, Florida, where the Prince was to play polo and attend a dinner with the Princess to raise money for the United World Colleges. This charity was started by the Prince's great-uncle, Lord Mountbatten and is supported by the Prince and his host in Palm Beach, the oil multimillionaire, Dr Armand Hammer.

The whole affair was dogged with rows, among them the discovery that the lady chairing the dinner was a former belly-dancer and that guests were paying $50,000 to dine with, and be photographed with the royals.

The Prince decided to take on the critics. In a speech at the dinner he hit back: 'What I want to know is what actually is wrong with being elite, for God's sake?'

The Princess of Wales at the dinner in Washington given in honour of the royal couple by the British Ambassador and his wife. The Princess is wearing a cream evening dress with her pearl and diamond tiara, a wedding present from the Queen.

And 'how on earth do they expect us to get anything done without money?'

He went on: 'How are we to have any hope of balanced and civilized leadership in the future unless there are some people who have learned about service to others, about compassion, about understanding, as far as is humanly possible, the other man's religion, the other man's customs, and his history, about courage to stand up for things that are noble, and for things that are true?

'After all, there's so much to be done in this world – so much famine exists, so much disease, so much poverty, so much conflict, bigotry and prejudice, and there are so many people who are crying out for help, for their own simple dreams to come true.'

In its way, it was the central thought that guided his year.

When the RAF VC10 took off from Palm Beach for home there

was great relief that the tour had gone so well despite the busy programme, possibly too busy in retrospect, and all the security worries.

Only three months later the Prince was back in the United States, this time in Texas and California and this time on his own. It was never explained exactly why the Princess did not go as well, but it may not be just a coincidence that the tour was at the same time as Prince William's school half-term break.

To judge by the news coverage the point of the tour of Texas was to meet J.R. and to hold up Texan symbols such as cowboy boots and hats. In fact, the State of Texas wanted help to celebrate its 150th anniversary, the Prince wanted to help to promote British trade with Texas, and his charities grossed $3 million in the process. It may have quelled any doubts that the Prince was a big draw in his own right.

On pages 92 and 93: The Princess of Wales posing with members of the Vienna Boys' Choir after attending a concert in her honour at the Augarten Palais in Vienna.

Below: The Prince and Princess of Wales posing for a photograph with members of their Austrian motorcycle escort.
Facing page above: The Prince and Princess of Wales saying goodbye to staff at the British Embassy Residence where they had stayed during their three days in Vienna.

The Princess joined him to help to promote British trade when they visited Austria for British Week in Vienna. Naturally, they met many Austrians – and many British firms selling goods to Austria. The Prince was chatted up by the pretty wife of the Mayor of Vienna and went to his first fashion show.

If that is an image of the Prince of Wales that the British like – the attractive, businesslike Prince – a few months later another side of his character was to draw some barbed comments. A speech of his was widely reported as one to an audience of Canadian lumberjacks. In fact, it was the opening of an arts festival, in the city of Prince George, British Columbia. And after his usual remarks about the warmness of the wel-

come and the weather, the Prince ventured on to the artistry on display at the festival for the next few days. He told the participants not to worry if they did not win any of the competitions because it was taking part that mattered. He went on:

'I would just say one more thing and that is that I rather feel that deep in the soul of mankind there is a reflection as on the surface of a mirror, of a mirror-calm lake of the beauty and harmony of the universe. But so often that reflection is obscured and ruffled by unaccountable storms. So much depends, I think, on how each one of us is introduced to and made aware of that reflection within us. So, I believe we have a duty to our children to try to develop this awareness, for it seems

Below left: The Prince and Princess of Wales' Household travelling in an airport bus on the way to board Concorde at the end of the visit to Vienna.
Below right: The Princess of Wales on board Concorde during the return journey from Vienna. This was the Princess's first flight on Concorde.

to me that it is only through the development of an inner peace in the individual, and through the outward manifestation of that reflection, that we can ever hope to attain the kind of peace in this world for which so many yearn. And we must strive if we can to make living into an art itself, although it will always remain a tremendous struggle.'

The speech is one of the best insights into the Prince's philosophy, which has been influenced by a wide range of sources from Kurt Hahn, the founder of his school, Gordonstoun through Jungian psychology, to the man

he chose as a godfather for Prince William, Sir Laurens van der Post. There is no doubt that the words are his own. He spends a great deal of time on his speeches and the mobile office word processor allows him to make changes up to the last minute.

The media that then went on ahead to Japan, in order to be there in good time for the royal arrival, were to miss one of the biggest stories of the year for royal-watchers, the Princess's fainting fit in Vancouver. So alarmed was the editor of one popular London newspaper that his royal reporter was in mid-air, that he tried unsuccessfully to get the airplane turned back back to Canada. It was also considered great luck by the royal household that very few pictures of the actual fainting exist. Considering the large press corps that follows the royal couple on foreign tours, and even allowing for those who had gone ahead to Japan, it is something of a miracle, or a disaster, depending on the point of view, that all that exists is a television shot of the Princess being helped away but still on her feet. In fact, she never did touch the ground; one of her aides saw that she was just about to go and, in a combined effort with the Prince of Wales, caught her in time.

Not surprisingly, it all sparked off more talk of the Princess not eating enough and the tour being too tiring. There being no analysis of fainting fits by royal princesses, nobody will ever know the real cause. The royal tour of British Columbia was very hectic and the tours of the various national pavilions of

Expo 86, most of them overheated and badly ventilated, placed an additional strain on top of an already overcrowded schedule.

As to the other possible cause, not eating enough, anybody who has seen the Princess swim or dance could not suggest that watching her weight was a problem. But the disruption of meals that happens with jet lag, and the exertion of a busy tour, are a dangerous combination.

Above: The Prince and Princess of Wales leaving Christ Church Cathedral, Vancouver during the Royal Tour of British Columbia in May 1986. Later in the same day they flew to Prince George in the province's interior to plant a spruce tree and open an arts festival.
Facing page: The Prince and Princess applauding a dance by Musqueam Indians at Expo 86, the world fair organized by Vancouver to celebrate its centenary.
Below: On board the ferry Queen of the North at Nanaimo on Vancouver Island.

Above: The Prince of Wales inspecting the guard of honour during the official welcoming ceremony at the Akasaka Palace in Tokyo. He is accompanied by the Prime Minister of Japan, Mr Yasuhiro Nakasone and behind, by his Equerry, Lieutenant-Colonel Brian Anderson.

Facing page above: The Princess of Wales at the colourful welcoming ceremony in Tokyo.
Facing page below: The five-day tour of Japan by the Prince and Princess of Wales in May 1986 captured the imagination of the ordinary Japanese who crowded the streets of Tokyo throughout their visit in the hope of catching a glimpse of the royal couple.

Though it hurt her self-confidence for a time, it did not ruin the tour of Japan that followed. The visit still holds very happy memories for the Prince and Princess. They were reassured by the presence of Prince Hiro as a host; they had met him while he was studying in England.

Asked what struck him most about Japan on his visit, the Prince says:

'I had been before in 1970 and so I had some idea about the country already but I think the most intriguing thing about Japan is the extraordinary relationship between the ancient, traditional past and their new, highly efficient technological existence. It is absolutely fascinating to see the one side by side

with the other. But, of course, the technological revolution has happened in a very short timescale and has been imposed on a very traditional society.

'My theory, for what it is worth, is that they have been such a success in industrial terms and in terms of looking after their workforce, and at which they're so brilliant, because the original, traditional society had the same concept of looking after people. Somehow, it has been able to move from the traditional into the modern society much more easily perhaps than in Europe where we had this very long and complex period of industrial revolution.

'I think we can to a certain extent learn something from the

Above: More than 100,000 people lined the streets of Tokyo in scenes of near hysteria to catch a glimpse of the Prince and Princess of Wales as they passed by in their open car.

Facing page: The Princess of Wales and a little Japanese boy wait for the Prince outside St Alban's Anglican church in Tokyo.

Japanese; in particular, the way in which they manage people and there is no doubt about it that when they come over here and set up factories, whether television or car factories, that the British workforces do find them extremely good to work for.'

In his speech to the Japanese

Parliament, the Prince said that, despite the friendship between Japan and Britain, he could not help feeling that we do not know the Japanese as well as they know us. He said that they had spent a century getting to know and understand us, so perhaps we should try harder to study their

Above: The Prince of Wales addressing the National Diet, the Japanese Parliament, in Tokyo. The Prince spoke at length about the closer cooperation that should take place between Britain and Japan. Of the tour he said: 'We will gather many fond memories and will, in turn, pass them on to our children, in the hope that our two countries will grow closer together in mutual understanding and partnership.'
Facing page: The Princess of Wales in a sapphire-blue evening dress for the audience with Emperor Hirohito of Japan. After the audience the Emperor and other members of the imperial family were hosts to the Prince and Princess at a sumptuous court banquet.

language, history, culture, civilization and customs.

In the short tour lasting only a few days he and the Princess set about just that. Tea ceremonies, silk kimonos, sumo wrestling,

Buddhist temples, flower-arranging, Japanese food – all were tried and tested. The Prince spoke to businessmen trading with Britain, and to the 'young achievers' of Japanese society.

Right: One of the Princess's engagements in a busy schedule was a visit to the Red Cross Hospital Infants' Home in Tokyo.

PUBLIC DUTIES

A terraced house in Bedford Row in central London is the base for many of the Prince's charities. It is a network of financially separate but interlocking groups.

The Royal Jubilee Trusts, the Prince's Trust, Youth Business Initiative, and The Prince of Wales' Advisory Group on Disability share the building. Some people find all the different names rather confusing, but the aim is to set up a 'super-trust' while at the same time honouring the wishes of those who gave money to the specific trusts for particular reasons.

The confusion is further increased by the existence of a totally separate Prince of Wales' Charities Trust, which distri-butes money to a wide range of causes.

The best-known name is probably the Prince's Trust, which has collected a lot of money from pop concerts given by supporters of the Trust's aims. In the summer of 1986 at Wembley Arena, the biggest names in British pop music, including Paul McCartney, Mick Jagger and David Bowie, brought the audience, including the Prince and Princess, to their feet time and again.

The history of the Trust goes back to 1972 when the Prince began thinking of ways that young people who felt alienated from society could be helped to help themselves. In 1976 he formally established the Trust, and the recruitment began of

On page 110: The Princess of Wales has many interests in her public life, one of the principal ones being children. Here, she is talking to a physically handicapped child during a visit to the Markfield Project in London in March 1986.
On page 111: The Prince of Wales chairing a meeting of the Royal Jubilee Trusts' Administrative Council in December 1985. The Royal Jubilee Trusts is made up of The Queen's Silver Jubilee Trust whose aim is to help young people help others of any age in the community and King George's Jubilee Trust which provides financial support for youth projects. The Administrative Council is made up of staff from the central headquarters in London, representatives from local committees and people from all aspects of the community.

hundreds of volunteers to help to provide small grants and support for schemes for young people.

These grants are awarded to young people between the ages of fourteen and twenty-five who are disadvantaged socially or economically, or who are physically handicapped. They have to come up with their own ideas for self-help. The average grant is £200 and the total now given out each year is £250,000.

Asked about the Prince's Trust and whether he had a master plan, the Prince says:

'I don't think I have a master plan but basically, I want to see the Prince's Trust as my fighting arm, incorporating some of my other trusts and organizations under a kind of umbrella. But the great thing about the Prince's Trust, I feel, is that it should remain flexible in its terms of reference because that way I think it's easier to respond to the various situations as they arise throughout the country.

'For instance, one might suddenly decide that there was a particular area that you wanted to tackle, that needed tackling and that the Prince's Trust is a good way of doing so because we can try pilot schemes here and pilot schemes there. If some don't work we abandon them, if others work we obviously pursue them, but this is what we did when setting up the Youth Business Initiative in the wake of those Toxteth riots in 1981.

'I felt very strongly that unemployment and the problems created by large numbers of young people being out of work for long periods of time was an area in which the Trust ought to get involved while it lasted and to try and see what we could do, very often as a mere pinprick in terms of the whole problem throughout the country. That's the great thing, for me, anyway, the Prince's Trust, remaining flexible and being able to tackle different problems.'

Right and facing page: One of the Prince of Wales' main interests is the Prince's Trust which was established in 1976 on his personal initiative to encourage young people to help themselves. Film premières, gala performances and pop concerts attended by the Prince and Princess are some of the ways of raising funds for the Trust. (Right) The Prince of Wales talking to Rod Stewart at the 10th Anniversary Concert at Wembley in June 1986. (Facing page above left) The Princess of Wales at the Supertramp concert at the Royal Albert Hall in London in March 1986. (Facing page above right) The Princess of Wales at the film première of 'Back to the Future' in December 1985.

At the start the Prince told the Trust staff he was prepared to take risks and that it was perhaps inevitable that one day someone might run off with the money, but even that should not stop the Trust taking chances. He has also said that they must always try to get the money to the recipient as quickly as possible and to avoid all delay and bureaucratic red tape.

The Prince has been determined not to be put off by the problems. In 1986 the Prince's Trust hired a holiday camp at Great Yarmouth in eastern England to give young unem-ployed the chance to develop skills that they might not nor-mally have the chance to do: everything from computers to scuba diving. But one night part of the camp was vandalized. When the Prince visited the camp a few days later, he went on the counter-attack, saying that he had been told the damage was done by outsiders and accusing the press of exaggeration. He commented:

'I think it is rather depressing, actually, how the media can be-have on these occasions. Always wanting to pick up the negative side of things, always wanting to

The Princess of Wales cutting the birthday cake at the 10th Anniversary Concert of the Prince's Trust, watched by Phil Collins and Tina Turner. Many well-known rock stars came together in this spectacular concert to raise funds for the Trust.

find a failure, and, not only that, exaggerate the whole thing out of all proportion to what actually went on. I think a lot of people in the press bear a very serious responsibility for behaving like this. One reporter was told to write a story about the whole thing being full of yobs and people smashing beer cans. That, I think, is indicative of the kind of standards we have all come to expect now from the newspapers.'

To help to rekindle business initiative the Prince's Trust set up a special scheme in March 1982 to give grants to unemployed young people up to the age of twenty-five, to help them to prepare to start up their own businesses. The Youth Business Initiative, as it is known, has

launched schemes in ten areas of Britain with the highest unemployment. Successful applicants receive not only money but professional advice, training and support.

On business initiative the Prince says:

'It seems to me that one of the great problems we face in this country is the death of so many of our traditional industries and the rise of our competitors in terms of those who've managed to innovate and re-equip quicker than ourselves, which has, I think, helped to put an awful lot of people out of work.

'We need, I think, a new industrial revolution, because only that way, through starting off small businesses, it seems to me, can you eventually arrive at a

The Prince of Wales, President, with Lord Remnant, Chairman, at the Royal Jubilee Trusts' Administrative Council meeting in December 1985. This meeting takes place once a year and is chaired by the Prince whenever he is able to attend.

situation where the small businesses become bigger ones and employ more people.'

The Prince strongly believes that small businesses are the way to create jobs. He is president of an organization called Business in the Community and a great many of his engagements are visits to advice centres for small businesses. He greatly enjoys hearing the problems of those starting up and those who help them. At Leith in Edinburgh he and the Princess met a couple starting a business putting clocks in pieces of Scottish rock. The Prince said one clock looked like a chunk that had been taken out of Balmoral.

The Prince encapsulated his beliefs about business enterprise in an off-the-cuff speech at an enterprise centre in London:

'I fundamentally believe that there is an enormous amount of talent, skill, ingenuity and enthusiasm waiting there to be unlocked, unleashed and freed from cloying red tape. I know that

there have to be rules and regulations and everything else but the whole spirit and survival and regeneration of this country depend on it, because without that flexibility and imagination I don't believe we're going to get anywhere and we will become the poor man of Europe, and I will say it again, a fourth-rate nation.'

The Prince has become a great admirer of the enterprise culture in the United States and advocates the American idea of large companies contributing a percentage of their profits to local concerns.

But there is two-way traffic across the Atlantic. A group of Americans, 'Jobs for Youth' of Boston, have visited Britain to see how Youth Business Initiative works. Comparing experiences, the Prince told them: 'It's built, in a sense, into the American ethos, this business of starting off on your own, a little bit more than it is in this country. But I think one of the things we find in this country is that in the north of England there's no tradition at all of individual enterprise. It has all been very much based on the traditional big industries.'

The Prince has another idea, too, to help the unemployed in Sunderland, on the north-east coast of England, where he is running an experiment. The Prince of Wales' Community Venture is meant to encourage young people to give service to their community. Four teams of Venturers are trained each year in community work, ranging from first aid to the Fire Brigade, from helping in a spastics home to adventure training in Wales. The project is typical of the Prince's style. He has raised the money from voluntary organizations, the Venturers' Van is lent by a local dealer and one of the scheme's administrators is on loan from a bank. The Prince has visited the scheme twice this year and writes notes of encouragement to the staff and Venturers.

When he talks with the young trainees, he seems genuinely shocked that a girl of twenty-two should have been unemployed for four years of her life. He says: 'I believe that we should all have the opportunity at one stage in our lives to make a contribution to our community. It is also vital that we find ways in which people from all walks of life and backgrounds can operate together for a limited period in their lives. Ours is one of the very few countries where this does not happen.'

The Prince has his critics. They say he is something of an oddball, an eccentric. But the people who work with him on these schemes are impressed by his dedication and hard work. They sense his concern that more is not being done about Britain's social and economic problems. The Prince has put it this way:

'Sometimes I get frustrated that I can't do more about it, because it is a gigantic problem and anything we do, either through

Right: The Prince of Wales presenting the Stone Federation's 1985 design awards for natural stone at the Royal Institute of British Architects

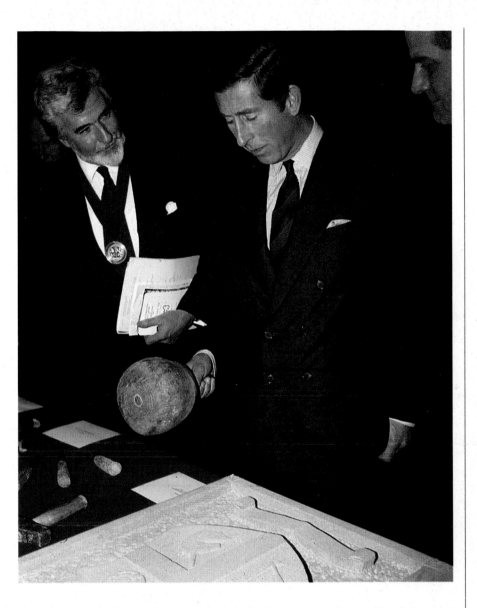

Facing page: The Prince of Wales attends a reunion of HMS Kelly veterans. His great-uncle, Lord Mountbatten was captain of the ship when it sank during the Second World War. The Prince is now President of the HMS Kelly Reunion Association.

straight Prince's Trust grants or through the Youth Business Initiative, starting people off in their own enterprise, is a mere pin-prick in terms of the whole problem. But I always get encouraged by people I meet and the enthusiasm of the young once they have been introduced to the possibilities that exist.'

Another part of the Prince's plan for business regeneration is Community Architecture. Again, this has been represented as a faintly confusing or even crackpot idea. In fact, rebuilding areas to make them better to live in is a way of creating jobs and giving people a better lifestyle.

In late 1985 the Prince was said to have fallen out with a leading proponent of Community Architecture, Rod Hackney, after a newspaper article quoted Hackney quoting the Prince. By June 1986 they were on the same platform at the Community Enterprise Scheme awards. The Prince explained his interest in Community Enterprise and Community Architecture:

'Some people may think, I suspect, that it's a passing fad or a passing fashion but I don't think

Below left: As well as being Prince of Wales the Prince is also Duke of Cornwall and in April 1986 he paid a two-day visit to the Isles of Scilly, much of which is owned by the Duchy. The coat of arms of the Duke of Cornwall shows besants, gold coins brought back by the Crusaders, surmounted by the coronet of the Heir Apparent.
Below right: The Duchy Office on the Isles of Scilly.

it is. I know, for instance, that there is nothing worse than the over-zealous convert. You may see that before you, but I am totally aware of the difficulties of being over-enthusiastic about one particular line to take. I have, myself, seen the effect on people as individuals that these schemes produce, and I'm afraid it's very difficult to remain quiet about it because I've found it's so enormously inspiring. So it gave me enormous encouragement to feel that these sort of things were possible, but I believe that an enormous number of people in this country had no idea of what was going on. So I find I just simply can't ignore this effect that these kinds of community projects have on people.'

He took his audience through his own experience visiting schemes around the country before ending with an habitual theme: 'To restore hope we must have a vision and a source of inspiration, we must sink our differences and cut great swathes through the cat's cradles of red tape which choke this country from end to end.'

As he tours the country the Prince gets a good response to his ideas from sometimes unlikely quarters. In July 1986 he visited Handsworth in Birmingham, where a year before two people had been killed in riots. He was welcomed, not as a symbol of the white establishment, but as the man whose charity had helped to start a fashion firm run by local Rastafarians, and had assisted two Birmingham pop groups.

The local black radio called him 'the caring Prince, the man who don't just talk, who acts'; and on a walkabout in Deptford, in south-east London, in July 1986 a young black told him repeatedly: 'You are the man, you are the man, the whole black community is proud of you.' It was perhaps this kind of welcome that encouraged the Prince on this visit to pop into a pub at the end of the street. By chance, it was called the Windsor Castle, though it is unlikely that there is anything quite like it in the State

Apartments. It was an impromptu touch that helped his image.

There are other charities close to the Prince's heart outside the general umbrella of the Prince's Trust. Among them is Operation Raleigh, an international charity which sends young people to help in developing countries. The Prince's visit to Palm Springs, California, was to raise funds for this cause. On this occasion he found time, as he does on many foreign tours, to meet young venturers just leaving for or just returning from Operation Raleigh adventures. He found one young man who had heard of Operation Raleigh on an interview the Prince had given to American television. The young man had never heard of such an idea in the United States, and thought that joining the navy was too extreme.

Another young American the Prince met then was just back from the depths of Bolivia. The Prince wondered if there were times when he asked himself, 'Why am I doing this?' The young man told him there had been occasions such as when, walking in rivers with his feet getting wet for eight or nine hours, he started thinking, 'Why am I here?' But then he woke up in the morning and did it all over again.

Quite apart from his charities and trusts, being the heir to the throne and Duke of Cornwall is enough work in itself. When the Prince is asked in public about his role in life he sometimes appears hesitant. In private his frustration is not that he has no role, but that he has so many, and so many demands on his time, that his

efforts may be spread too thinly.

The Duchy of Cornwall is an example of the responsibilities he carries. The Duchy owns 130,000 acres in eleven counties, including 44 acres of Greater London, many of them around the Oval Cricket Ground in Kennington, London. And the landlord takes an active interest. The main point of his meeting with Rod Hackney on the Royal Train was not to discuss the state of Britain's inner cities but the state of Curry Mallet in Somerset. The Duchy owns nearly the whole village

The Duke of Cornwall talking to one of his tenant farmers on St Mary's, the Isles of Scilly. The Duke takes a close interest in the farms owned by the Duchy and has worked on two of them in the West Country in order to get a better knowledge of how they are run.

On pages 120 and 121: As well as his duties as Duke of Cornwall the Prince of Wales has ceremonial ones. On a few occasions, such as in March 1986, he has represented the Queen at investitures while she was abroad. These colourful ceremonies take place in the Ballroom at Buckingham Palace.

and the Prince discovered that over the years the locals were getting anxious about the housing there, and in particular the lack of housing for young people in the village.

The Prince went to the village to talk about their problems and found one thing they wanted was a village hall. He told Hackney on the train: 'It suddenly occurred to me that maybe there was a situation where we could use a community architect actually to get all the villagers together to find out exactly what they wanted.'

Once such ideas have been set in motion, the Prince monitors the progress. In the spring of 1986 he visited the Isles of Scilly, much of which is owned by the Duchy and where he has a bungalow, Tamarisk, on the island of St Mary's. He went to a flower farm, where the daffodils were being cut for market. The new tenant of the farm explained that there was a problem with the erosion of the cliff at the end of the field. He told the Prince: 'There's nothing much we can do about that.'

'Except watch to see your field disappear slowly,' said the Prince.

'Your field,' the tenant reminded his landlord.

In contrast to watching over the farms and villages of the Duchy, the Prince's position as heir to the throne carries with it many state ceremonial duties. These include attending state dinners for visiting foreign dignatories, and – when the Queen is abroad – presenting honours at the investitures at Buckingham Palace.

Above: The Prince of Wales awarding the accolade of knighthood at an investiture in March 1986

Facing page: The ceremonial duties carried out by the Prince of Wales mean a vast array of different uniforms and medals which are kept meticulously in the Uniform Room at Kensington Palace

These occasions combine the pageantry of the British monarchy, epitomized in the Yeomen of the Guard who are on duty, with informal touches when the Prince chats with those getting their awards.

Occasionally, investitures are held outside London. In the spring of 1986, while the Prince was visiting an Enterprise Centre in South Shields, Tyne and Wear,

he was asked to present an OBE to the author Catherine Cookson, who was too ill to travel to London. She is nearly eighty years old and her publishers say that she has sold 86 million books around the world.

An office in an Enterprise Centre was nothing like the Ballroom at the Palace but the ceremony was all the more personal for that. Their conversation shows the Prince's style in setting people at their ease on what can be nervous occasions.

The Prince: 'I hear you've got an enormous amount of novels in the pipeline?'

Catherine Cookson: 'Well, there's eight at the publishers waiting to come out.'

The Prince (in some surprise): 'Eight? How do you do it? Your head must be full of stories all the time, that are longing to get out.'

Catherine Cookson: 'If I live long enough to see them out.'

The Prince: 'I hope so, you've got to. When you learned your syntax and grammar, were they very strict up here when you were at school?'

Catherine Cookson: 'I hardly ever went to school!'

The Prince: 'Oh, well, I will give you this, which gives me enormous pleasure. I'm afraid I'm a very poor substitute for the Queen, but it's the least we can do, with many congratulations.'

Catherine Cookson: 'A very great day for me. I feel like Cinderella who's arrived at the ball.'

The two chatted on so much they even discovered that they suffered from the same complaint – nose bleeds.

Above: The Prince of Wales' valet, Ken Stronach cleaning the sword for the Number One naval uniform and the shoes to wear with his uniforms. Centre: Worn on the Number One naval uniform are: (Top left to right) The Queen's Service Order (New Zealand), the Queen's Coronation Medal and the Queen's Silver Jubilee Medal; (Below) The star of the Most Noble Order of the Garter and the star of The Most Ancient and the Most Noble Order of the Thistle. Left: The Prince in the uniform to greet the King and Queen of Spain in April 1986. Facing page: The Prince as Great Master of the Most Honourable Order of the Bath in May 1986.

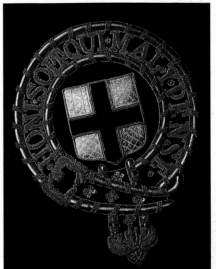

Above left: The Garter cap of black velvet and ostrich plumes. Top right: The Garter badge. Above right: The valet cleaning the Prince's boots. Left: The Prince of Wales' uniform and bearskin as Colonel of the Welsh Guards which he wears for the Queen's Birthday Parade in June.

Facing page: The Prince of Wales and Queen Elizabeth the Queen Mother at the service of the Most Noble Order of the Garter in June 1986. Apart from the addition of the black cap the Garter dress has hardly changed since the reign of Charles II in the seventeenth century.

Facing page: The Princess of Wales at the Barbican Centre in London to attend the Royal Academy of Music Gala Concert in May 1986. Both the Prince and Princess of Wales enjoy music and take an active interest in the music colleges in which they are involved. The Princess is President of the Royal Academy of Music and the Prince President of the Royal College of Music Centenary Appeal.

Right: The Prince of Wales said of his wife during their tour of Canada in May 1986: 'Little did she know that when she married me, she'd end up becoming involved with so many organizations and I think she really thought that it was a good excuse to be able to get through red traffic lights! But since then, she has taken on a large number of these concerns and given a great deal of time to them and I'm sure she will go on doing so for many years hence.' One of these concerns is the problem of drug abuse and in December 1985 she paid a visit to the staff of Customs and Excise at Heathrow Airport to see for herself the campaign against drug smuggling.

Year by year the Princess's workload has grown. In 1985 she undertook 299 public duties, compared with 177 the year before, when Prince Henry was born. Of her 206 engagements carried out in Britain, 106 were on her own.

The Prince, who not so long ago was being accused of losing interest in such duties, carried out 404 engagements in 1985, compared with 316 the previous year. Such figures are not foolproof; it is possible to do five short engagements in the same time as

Right: The Princess of Wales, Patron of Birthright, meeting the Three Degrees pop group at the Birthright Ball celebrating the charity's tenth anniversary

Right: The Princess of Wales at a drug addiction unit in Cardiff in March 1986. She has now visited a number of such treatment centres and said recently: 'We have a battle on our hands. It has to be waged on two fronts: prevention and cure'.

Facing page: The Princess of Wales, Patron of Help the Aged, at the launch of the Charity's Silver Jubilee Appeal in London in March 1986.

one long one. But league tables of royal engagements, except the one conducted every year by a reader of *The Times*, do not show the big workload imposed by overseas tours. The Court Circular itself only notes that the Prince and Princess of Wales left for abroad and returned a few weeks later.

The other change in the Princess's work has been the increased number of speeches she has made. Her first recorded speeches as Princess were very brief affairs at Cardiff City Hall and at a new post office near the Spencer family home in Northamptonshire. Both were delivered rather nervously and quickly.

In the spring of 1986 the Princess launched the Help the Aged Silver Jubilee Appeal, and warned of the dangers of drugs at the North East Council on Addiction in Newcastle. The speeches on both occasions were marked by a slower delivery, a cooler complexion, but still deep sighs of relief from the Princess once they were over.

Both speeches, too, were not in the easiest of settings. The Help the Aged reception in a London hotel was attended by celebrities from show business, experts in timing and delivery. And the room in Newcastle was far too small for all the reporters and guests who wanted to hear her. Remembering her fainting fit in Canada, her equerry and detective, Inspector Allan Peters, checked the room a few minutes before the Princess arrived and both looked uneasy. Windows were opened and guests asked to move back. Outside, the Princess was having last-minute nerves, but they never showed once she entered the room.

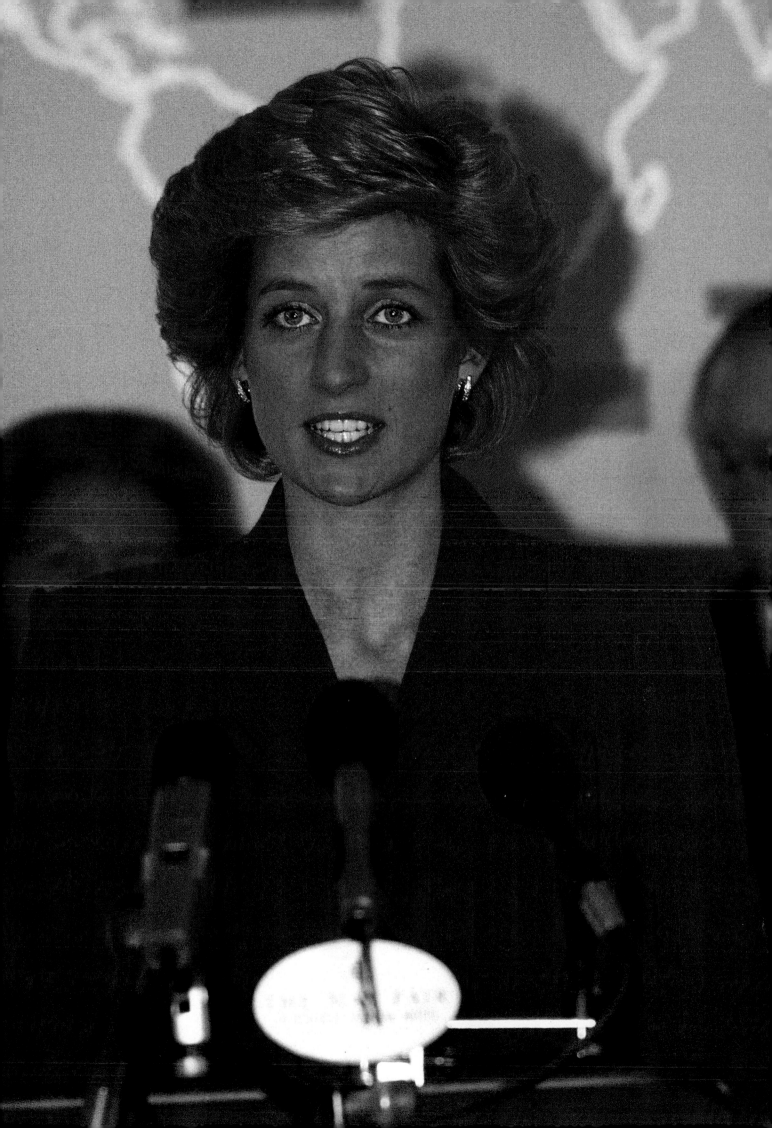

She told her audience that there was an increasing number of families in Britain which had some first-hand knowledge or experience of the despair, misery and sheer waste of life caused by drug addiction:

'We have a battle on our hands. It has to be waged on two major fronts: prevention and cure. As far as prevention is concerned, parents and teachers are in the front line. As a parent myself, I am only too aware of the responsibility this implies in terms of the kind of upbringing best suited to encourage the child to say "no".

'From the point of view of cure, it is vitally important to have adequate facilities available, such as those which allow ex-addicts to run homes or treatment centres for people who have made the decision to try to abandon drugs.'

During 1985 and 1986 the Princess visited a number of treatment centres and talked with drug addicts and those trying to help them. In Cardiff she met mothers trying to get off drugs, and talked of the effects on their children. She also talked to a former miner who became addicted to amphetomines because of problems at work and at home. He told her how he became addicted, where he got the drugs from and the effects of the treatment he was receiving.

The Princess's growing self-confidence allows her to talk freely with people without fear of saying the wrong thing. In the

Facing page: The Princess of Wales accompanies her husband on many engagements as well as carrying out more and more on her own. In April 1986 the Prince's injured finger led to the royal couple performing a double act in opening the new London Underground station and the new Terminal 4 building at Heathrow Airport. Afterwards the Prince and Princess toured the building and met check-in staff.

Below: In December 1985 the Princess of Wales presented the Children of Courage awards at Westminster Abbey. She met the ten children, including the youngest heart-lung transplant patient seen in her arms.

nine months since ITN began recording her conversations at work for the special programme about her and the Prince, those close to her have noticed the continuing change from the so-called 'Shy Di' to a self-assured young woman.

This is perhaps most clearly shown when she supports Help the Aged by visiting old people's homes. The Princess said at the Silver Jubilee Reception: 'Growing old is, sadly, not always fun. There are elderly people in this country who fear for their financial and physical security. Many are concerned about their health, many are frail and worried about living an independent life.'

Translating this concern into face-to-face conversations means chatting with old people about their problems and amusing them. It is not easy, but every little bit helps. So, an old woman in Surrey, discovered stuffing kneeling rests for churches, is asked by the Princess: 'It's not laddered tights going in there?'

Dr Barnardo's is one of the Princess's favourite charities. In March 1986 she met children who were hoping to be adopted and a couple who were adopting a four-month-old Down's syndrome baby. She heard how the couple had already fostered two children and two adult mentally-handicapped as well. In admiration, the Princess asked: 'Are you building an extension to your house?'

The Princess went to a Dr Barnardo's home in Belfast during her one-day visit to Northern Ireland in October 1985. A little girl who could not blow out the birthday candles got a helping hand and puff from the Princess. The Princess was also able to show her concern for the deaf on that visit. At a buffet lunch she used sign language to introduce herself to a group of deaf and dumb youths.

One of the most handicapped people she met in 1986 was at the Sheffield Spinal Injuries Centre.

Trevor Wright had dived into water that was too shallow. He had the worst kind of injury it is possible to have and still breathe. The Princess was told how he exercised his lungs by blowing through a tube into an old whisky bottle full of water.

To help the disadvantaged, the Princess now has her own Charities Trust, separate from the Prince's, so that she can turn her interest and concern into the kind of positive action that has so absorbed her husband. It is the partnership in being.

Above: The Princess paid a one-day visit to Northern Ireland in October 1985. Her busy schedule included planting a tree at Hillsborough Castle and visiting a Dr Barnardo's child care unit near Stormont. It was the home's fourth birthday and before leaving, the Princess helped a little girl blow out the candles.

Right: The Princess of Wales visiting the Spinal Injuries Unit in Sheffield. Facing page: The Princess of Wales wearing the British Red Cross uniform. She is Patron of the British Red Cross Society's Youth and Juniors.

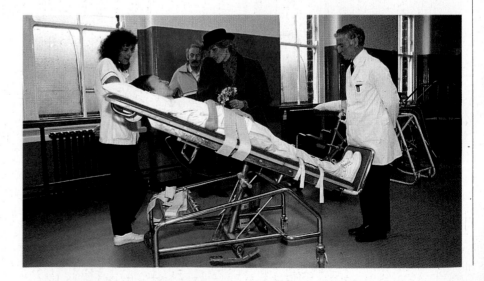

PRIVATE INTERESTS

After a foreign tour or a busy round of engagements in Britain, the Prince of Wales likes to sit in his walled garden at Highgrove. He says that he has put his heart and soul into creating it and he finds it 'enormously enjoyable'.

When the Prince bought the house in 1980 the walled garden was rather basic, with black cinder paths, many vegetables but few flowers, and a hole in one wall where somebody had made a gap to get a tractor through.

The Prince says that he had always wanted to create something special in a walled garden. 'When I first came to look at the house I did rather fall in love with it. And I'd always wanted to grow fruit, flowers and vegetables in one place.

'One of the great things was that as a wedding present we were given a complete set of fruit trees by the Fruiterers' Company and, believe it or not, a herb garden by the Sussex branch of the Women's Institute.'

The Prince says that his original plan was much too complicated, with all sorts of box-shaped beds and 'D's and 'C's. He thinks that it would have been spectacular but would have taken years to finish and hundreds of people to do it.

'So, in the end, I had simple crosses and St Andrew's crosses in four quarters, and a fountain in the middle, and arbours in the centre of each quarter, with roses, wisteria and clematis up them, to provide rather nice, cool, shady spots. And then two apple tun-

nels which in about ten years will look marvellous when they grow completely over.

'There's a gazebo against the wall to give the garden a central feature and on either side a sweet briar hedge because, apart from anything else, it smells fantastic and grows like Billy-O.'

The Prince says that he loves going to the garden and pottering about in it, sitting and reading.

'It is rather fun because it's one area in which perhaps it's possible to create something. As far as Highgrove is concerned there was basically nothing there when I arrived and so it has been a great

challenge to create something. It would be different, I think, if you arrived somewhere and found a really marvellous garden in existence, you could only make it worse; it's sometimes difficult to make it better. But, in this case, it's been my own particular feelings and ideas which have gone into it with help from other people who know about these things better than I do.

'But I love the business of planting my own plants and trees; I've done most of the planting there, with the help of my team, and as a result they're like, in a sense, one's own children. I go round and I examine them very carefully and see how they're getting on and occasionally talk to them, which I think is very important – they do respond in a funny way. And, of course, if they die I feel deeply saddened by that. But it's a remarkable thing

which I didn't realize I would develop because it was only when I had my own place that I actually became interested in it.'

Even the weeding?

'Even the weeding. Very therapeutic, weeding. And it's marvellous if you can do it enough to see the effect. But it's trying to keep up with the dead heading and all these other things which is problematical. I've got slight *folie de grandeur* – I have endless plans to do new things which is very exciting but I just like to leave something better than I found originally.'

And the Prince built, or rebuilt, his own gateway:

'I designed that rather Moorish arch, which actually was taken directly off one of the minarets on the Taj Mahal. I rather like, I love the arches, those Moorish arches, Indian arches. I know it's not always what some people like,

The walled garden at Highgrove which the Prince of Wales designed himself. Having rejected his first plan which was too complicated, the Prince decided upon 'simple crosses and St Andrew's crosses in four quarters, and a fountain in the middle, and arbours in the centre of each quarter, with roses, wisteria and clematis up them.'

but I rather like it. I like the shape as you look through it both ways.'

The Prince is very proud of the beans and sweet peas which he grows, not up the traditional sticks, but in the form of a tunnel. He says: 'It's rather fun because you can then walk down the tunnel picking the beans and flowers.'

The arbours are tranquil places. The Prince says it is 'fun to move down a path and then come to a rather shady spot which has masses of different scents and smells. You can sit there quietly if you want to, contemplating the infinite, and then move on to something else.'

That something else is often the herb garden. He says: 'It is so enjoyable because there is an awful lot to learn. There are some marvellous old books about what you can do with herbs. Also, it's rather amusing trying to invent new soups. I've never tried nettle

Dennis Brown, the gardener at Highgrove. The garden provides enough fresh vegetables for both homes of the Prince and Princess.

soup, for instance, which I'm told is quite good. And another herb called lovage makes interesting soup. I rather like cold soups and you can make very good ones that way.

'I was also thinking of trying to grow some wonderful old-fashioned vegetables like coloured cabbage.'

When the Prince is in the garden he sometimes finds his chefs there, collecting herbs or fresh vegetables from gardener Dennis Brown.

At present the garden is very much the Prince's own domain and he has yet to see which child takes to gardening. When they are a bit older he says he may set aside a little area for them to garden in. 'If you've got a little garden of your own it's rather fun to learn that way.'

As well as his walled garden the Prince is very fond of the wild-flower garden he has developed by the front drive into High-grove. And he has done a lot of work on areas such as the small spinney copse which he has been

trying to turn into a woodland garden. It was when doing this that he injured his finger badly. The Prince has been asked a number of times about just how he did it. He tells how he was driving a stake into the ground – and missed. He was taken to the casualty unit of the hospital in Swindon, where he found other casualties of weekend gardening and do-it-yourself work.

Fortunately for him the injury healed up before the start of the main English polo season. He spends many summer afternoons on the polo field and when he is on tour tries to fit in a game on some foreign field. To let him just turn up and ride different polo ponies, his polo manager, Major Ronald Ferguson, spends a few days before each match abroad testing the best available ponies in the area. His friendship with the Prince goes back many years, long before the Major's younger daughter became en-gaged to Prince Andrew.

The Prince thinks that having to adapt to different ponies

Polo tops the list of the Prince of Wales' off-duty activities and he plays regularly during the season as often as his many commitments permit. One of the teams he plays for regularly is Les Diables Bleus.

143

Facing page: The Prince of Wales talking to his polo manager, Major Ronald Ferguson in Melbourne, Australia during the Royal Tour of 1985. Whenever the Prince is scheduled to play a polo match abroad his polo manager accompanies the royal party in order to organize the ponies that Prince Charles will ride.

around the world is very good for his riding, and that he has learned a lot from his matches in Australia and the United States. Major Ferguson prepares a shortlist of ponies which the Prince tests a few days before the match, and he then makes his final selection. Sometimes, as in Palm Beach in Florida in November 1986, the Prince only has time to turn up and ride whichever ponies the Major has chosen.

But more often, as in Melbourne in November 1985, the Prince will use his morning off to 'stick and ball' with different ponies – that is riding around a practice field testing the reaction and abilities of each pony. 'The difficulty I always find is to tell if the pony is going to be good in an

actual game when you are just riding it stick and balling. It's very often a completely different thing and the best ponies very often are the ones that are worst when you try them.

'What is good for one person is not always good for another, and it's really a question of how handy each pony is, whether it runs and stops the way you want it to, and in a comfortable way. There are many ponies that bounce around and throw you out of the saddle, destroying all chances of a happily married existence if you're not careful. What you want ideally is a pony that is a lovely stable platform from which to hit and do things without worrying about what it's going to do.'

Right: The Princess of Wales at Werribee Park in Melbourne where she watched the Prince play polo and presented the prizes afterwards.
Far right: Prince Henry with the Shetland pony, Smokey at Highgrove. Both princes are learning to ride and may one day follow the Prince of Wales on to the polo field.

Facing page: The Princess of Wales at Highgrove with Prince Henry

Below left: Prince William jumping off Smokey into the arms of the groom, Marion Cox
Below right: Most years the Prince and Princess of Wales like to have a winter skiing holiday. In 1986 they travelled to Switzerland with some friends, including Miss Sarah Ferguson whose engagement to Prince Andrew was only a few weeks away, and skiied in and around Klosters and Davos.

Major Ferguson is very experienced in choosing ponies for the Prince. The Prince says of him: 'I think probably by now he has got the idea of what I like and what I don't like. He and I think the same about ponies, I suspect.' However good they are in selecting the ponies it is still up to the Prince's ability and fitness to make it a successful game.

When the Prince played in Melbourne in November 1985 it was his first game since August. He explains that his whole approach to life is to keep himself at least at minimum fitness. 'I can then suddenly go off and have a game of polo somewhere in the world or climb a mountain or go for a wind surf or something energetic. I try to do exercises every day, and not eat too much so that I can do these things which I enjoy. If I can't get the exercise I start clogging up, if you know what I mean.'

The Princess's way of avoiding clogging up is swimming and dancing. She has said that she would like to have been a dancer but was too tall. She showed her skills to a select audience when she danced with Wayne Sleep at a private Christmas concert at the Royal Opera House, Covent Garden. They had very little rehearsal time but it went smoothly. All the outside world was able to see were some rather fuzzy

Facing page: The Princess of Wales on the front steps of Highgrove with Prince Henry

Below and on the following pages: Relaxing at Highgrove with the children is one way in which the Prince and Princess of Wales spend their leisure time after the rigours of public life

photographs which one spectator gave to a daily newspaper.

The Princess has dancing lessons in London, and such is her interest in dancing that she sometimes goes to watch ballet rehearsals. She makes private visits to watch the London City Ballet, of which she is the patron. The artistic director, Harold King, wrote to the Princess asking her to be the patron and she agreed. She has got to know many of the dancers and, as well as watching them rehearse, she likes to sit with them afterwards, drink a papercupful of coffee from a machine and chat about the problems and pleasures of being a ballet dancer.

And there are occasionally problems, too, in being a patron.

She admitted that at a gala concert she had been suffering from a heavy cold: 'Every time there was a quiet note I'd go "cough, cough" and you know when you're not supposed to cough, you cough more.'

They liked that. Most people do not look for great eloquence or high purpose, but for the human touch and the human appreciation of themselves and the jobs they do. These are the moments, beyond the ceremonies and the speeches, that stay in people's minds and are relived with families and friends and neighbours. The Prince always says that his schemes and Trusts do little enough to solve big problems. But the human touch is always a multiplier.